To All Children in the World, Jesus said

"Let the little children come to me and do not hinder them, for to such belongs the kingdom of heaven."

~ Matthew 19:14

12 Keys to Having a Good Relationship with God

Published by Discover Media	www.discover.org.au
Inspired by	Alexis Bethany Cioccolanti
Written by	Steve Cioccolanti
Edited by	Caren Chung
Cover art and illustrations by	Gabriel Mutiara, Kiko Arakawa, Selena Sok, Rebekah Lin and Steve Cioccolanti
Layout design by	Steve Cioccolanti

ISBN 978-0-9873617-4-5   Printed in U.S.A.

12 Keys

to a Good
Relationship with God

Table of Contents

Preface

Alexis is my 6-year-old daughter. She loves to attend church and enjoys studying at a Christian school, but she realized not everyone has a relationship with God just because they go to church or attend a Christian school. A lot of adults dismiss the idea that children can get saved and have a good relationship with God from a young age. Parents send children to "children's church" or "Christian class" but don't expect children to get answers from prayer or impact other children's lives through miracles and healing.

Alexis wondered if it's possible for her to find out who God really is for herself and help other children get their own answers. She was thrilled to discover 12 keys that open up amazing and supernatural experiences with God. Inspired by conversations with Alexis, I wrote some of her ideas into a book so that parents and children can benefit from them. I have combined her thoughts with my thoughts, but in order to give readers a feel of how I experienced hearing some of these ideas from Alexis, I have written the book in her voice.

Introduction

My father Pastor Steve, I call him "Papa", wrote a book dedicated to me called "The Divine Code from 1 to 2020." It is a book about numbers. My first book is about 12 keys in the Bible. God has many keys to help you solve the difficulties of life.

I'd like to dedicate my first book to my Papa. I hope you will enjoy it. The keys are from God.

1. The Word of God

The Word of God is like a letter from God. We do not get many letters nowadays because everyone is sending emails. That makes letters very special. On the first day of school, my Papa wrote me a letter. I won't tell you everything, but just a bit: "Dear Daughter Alexis, If you will listen well and obey, you will learn many things. I'm proud of you. Love, Papa." After my first day at school, I told him, "This is the best day ever!"

Another time Papa put a letter in my schoolbag. This is a part of what it says: "Listen to your teachers the first time they speak and try to learn the names of the other students, just like you want them to know your name. I love you, Papa."

Letters are special. That's what the Bible is! I get to read a letter from God everyday.

——— God's Word ———

Proverbs 4:20-22
20 My son, be attentive to my words; incline your ear to my sayings. 21 Let them not escape from your sight; keep them within your heart.
22 For they are life to those who find them, and healing to all their flesh.

The Bible is important because it has healing. Everybody needs to be healed. When I feel sick, I put the Bible first. I tell my Papa, "I want to eat, but first I want to read my Bible chapter!" Bible sentences are called verses. I like taking turns with my Papa to read the Bible, he reads the odd verses (like 1, 3, 5) and I read the even verses (like 2, 4, 6). Every time we read the Bible together, I get better.

The Bible is interesting because we can learn more about God and about the old times before we were born! The Bible tells us how the world started. God is the Creator. He created the universe and filled it with life in six days, then on the seventh day He rested. That is why we have seven days in a week. The Bible even tells us some of our ancestors' names, important people like Adam and Eve, Noah and his three sons. When I read about how God helped other people and solved their problems, I have faith He can do the same things for me.

———— God's Word ————
Romans 10:17
So faith comes from hearing, and hearing through the word of Christ.

🌺 2. The Name of Jesus 🌺

The Name of Jesus is not like any other name. When we call on the Name of Jesus, we are born again. We can shout out His Name in troubled times and in good times. When I feel afraid I just say "Jesus!" He is always there for me. When you're not sure what to do, just say the Name of "Jesus" and God will be there for you.

——— The Name ———

John 14:13-14

13 Whatever you ask in my name, this I will do, that the Father may be glorified in the Son. 14 If you ask me anything in my name, I will do it.

Jesus' Name helped me be born again. When I was 3 years old, I believed Jesus and I prayed in Jesus' Name. That's how I got born again. When we believe Jesus' Name has power, we are born again.

When people inside a house believe in Jesus' Name, it's like God sits on top of our house, but the house doesn't break, the roof doesn't even collapse.

Jesus' Name brings good things over a house like joy, peace, blessing and protection. But if people deny Jesus, it's like the devil sits on top of their house. He brings bad things on them like hatred, sickness and anger.

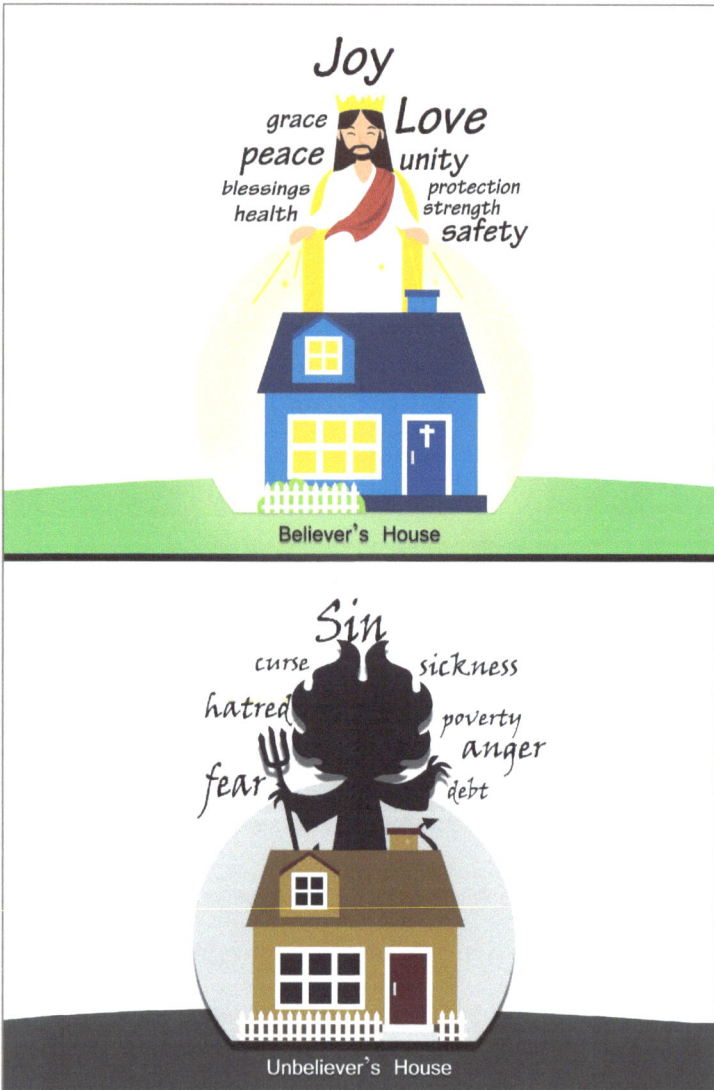

Joy

grace Love

peace unity

blessings protection

health strength

safety

Believer's House

Sin

curse sickness

hatred poverty

anger

fear debt

Unbeliever's House

There was a man in the Bible who was sick since he was born, and two Christians named Peter and John prayed for him in Jesus' Name. He believed and did what Peter told him. He got up and was healed! And Peter had to explain to the crowd what happened.

The Name

Acts 3:12, 16

12 ...why do you wonder at this, or why do you stare at us, as though by our own power or piety we have made him walk? ...
16 And his name—by faith in his name—has made this man strong whom you see and know, and the faith that is through Jesus has given the man this perfect health in the presence of you all.

In our church, we have kids' church and it's called "Mighty Minions". One time my friend Freesia was carried into kids' church by her dad, she was limping really badly. Her dad told us she had sprained her ankle that day. I asked the teacher if it was okay to pray for Freesia. Freesia agreed and the teacher was happy, so I kneeled on the floor in front of Freesia, laid my hands on Freesia's ankle, and I prayed something like this, "God, by Your stripes, Freesia was healed. Please help her right ankle so she can walk, jump and run, in Jesus' Name."

The teacher then asked Freesia if she felt any pain and she said no. He asked her to jump on one leg (the one that was sore), and she still said she felt no pain. Then he told all of us kids to praise Jesus for healing Freesia! I prayed in Jesus' Name and someone got healed! Freesia was walking and playing with us like normal! God is so good and He healed her because of Jesus' Name. I will never forget it.

You can call on the Name of Jesus any time. You can use His Name, sing His Name and shout out Jesus! In prayer or worship I sometimes do that. You can try it out.

3. The Holy Spirit

The Holy Spirit is really amazing. He helped Jesus do everything on earth, like heal people and go through difficult situations. The Holy Spirit even raised Jesus from the dead. No one had ever done that before!

——— The Holy Spirit ———

Romans 8:11

If the Spirit of him who raised Jesus from the dead dwells in you, he who raised Christ Jesus from the dead will also give life to your mortal bodies through his Spirit who dwells in you.

When Jesus rose again, He had all power in Heaven and on Earth. He didn't need the Holy Spirit as much as we do. So when Jesus went up to prepare a place for us in Heaven, He allowed the Holy Spirit to live inside us and guide us.

——— The Holy Spirit ———

John 16:13

When the Spirit of truth comes, he will guide you into all the truth, for he will not speak on his own

---

The Holy Spirit can help us understand what others might think or help us see what is happening in different places. It's not too hard for Him. With Him you'll know a little bit ahead about your day. You can know when something bad might be happening in another country. One time at "power prayer," which is a time our church friends come to pray at our house, one person felt very sad. The Holy Spirit showed her something sad was going to happen soon, and right after that the bad guys shot many people in Paris, France. Because we got together to pray, I'm sure God saved some people and less people got hurt. The Holy Spirit can tell you things you've never known about.

God gave us so many ways to defeat the devil, but it doesn't work if you don't pray. When I get up in the morning, I like to say, "Good morning, Holy Spirit!". When I pray in English, I pray for things that I know about. When I don't know and want the Holy Spirit's help, I pray in the Spirit.

On my way to school, I spend a little time praying in the Spirit with my family. It helps me hear God before school. Sometimes He tells me in my spirit, God loves me or God is very pleased with us.

🌺 4. The Blood of Jesus 🌺

One of my favorite children's books is called "The Lamb" by John R. Cross (published by Goodseed International). I read it many times. This book explains why Jesus is called "the Lamb of God," because in the old days lambs were sacrificed to "cover" people's sins. When Adam and Eve sinned and saw they were naked, God killed animals and "covered" their nakedness with animal skins.

Before Jesus came, people who believe in God would put their hands on a lamb's head. That is like

placing their sins on the lamb. Then, the lamb would be killed for their sins on a special place of death called an "altar". But animal sacrifices did not stop people from sinning. People were still bad in their hearts. Animal sacrifice was only a picture of what Jesus Christ would come to do for us.

When John the Baptist saw Jesus, his cousin John said, "Behold, the Lamb of God, who takes away the sin of the world!" (John 1:29) I think it's funny John did not say, "Behold, my cousin!" which is what I would have said. John saw something most people didn't see. Only Jesus' sacrifice on the Cross can take away our sins.

Jesus' Blood is greater than a lamb's blood. Jesus' Blood represents His pure and sinless life which is very precious. The Blood of Jesus saves us from sin and death. It's very similar to Jesus' Name.

The Blood

1 John 1:7
But if we walk in the light, as he is in the light, we have fellowship with one another, and the blood of Jesus his Son cleanses us from all sin.

The difference between the Name of Jesus and the Blood of Jesus is Jesus did not have to sacrifice Himself to give us His Name. But to give us His Blood, Jesus had to sacrifice Himself. No one likes to bleed. Jesus bled His Blood so you can be clean again, like when you were first made by God in Heaven.

The Blood of Jesus can be used for lots of things. It saves, it protects, and it heals. You can pray using the Blood of Jesus. The devil is very fearful of the Blood of Jesus because the Blood defeated him.

———— The Blood ————

Revelation 12:11 (AKJV)

And they overcame him because of the blood of the Lamb, and because of the word of their testimony…

My Papa pleads the Blood of Jesus over my brother and me. At school, we sing an old song by Lewis Jones called "There Is Power in the Blood". The chorus, the part that repeats, goes like this: "There is power, power, wonder-working power in the blood of the Lamb." It's really true! Whenever I take communion, I remember the Blood of Jesus.

5. The Body of Jesus

Did you know the body of Jesus was broken before He died? The Bible says, "By his wounds you have been healed" (1 Peter 2:24). Can you believe it? Jesus took our sins in His Blood and He took our sicknesses in His Body.

Jesus had the power to run away from people who were trying to hurt Him, but He let them beat His Body, so that He can take our pain and disease. Jesus sacrificed His body for you, so you can be healed every time you get sick.

One way to take the Body of Jesus is through communion. The bread that we eat during communion represents the Body of Jesus. It is not only to fill your tummy, but to remember God, that His Body was broken for you. Taking the Body of Jesus can heal you. If we haven't received Jesus into our heart, but we want to take the communion bread to fill our tummy, it isn't good and it will mean nothing. But if you take it properly, and you remember that His body was broken for your sickness, you can be healed.

The Body of Christ means another thing - all the people who go to church! They are also a key to having a good relationship with God. It's great to go to church services, but getting along with people might be hard. We have to learn to forgive when someone hurts us. "Forgive" means we stop blaming others.

The Body

1 Corinthians 11:29-31

29 For anyone who eats and drinks without discerning the body eats and drinks judgment on himself. 30 That is why many of you are weak and ill, and some have died. 31 But if we judged ourselves truly, we would not be judged.

When my brother Austin and I hurt each other, one of us has to say "Sorry!" and the other person has to say "I forgive you!" Or if both of us did something wrong, then both of us have to say "Sorry!", and both of us have to forgive each other, then we are friends again. We should not wait until our parents correct us.

The Body

1 John 4:20

If anyone says, "I love God," and hates his brother, he is a liar; for he who does not love his brother whom he has seen cannot love God whom he has not seen.

This means we should love someone just the way we would love God. If we did that, we would have a good life. Bad things happen to us when we don't love, because love is the most important thing to having a good relationship with God.

6. The Angels of God

All children have angels with them. Angels help us with our life. Our angels always see the face of God the Father.

We have many experiences with angels in our family. Angels help protect us because God sent angels so we can be safe. One time when my parents were sleeping, I climbed up a shelf and it started to tumble down. Then the angel saved me by rolling me over, so the shelf did not hit me in the head, just on my leg. Thank God I can still walk. Then Papa came to save me by moving the shelf away. It was amazing.

Once we lost our phone in Sydney. We looked on "Find my iPhone" (a map finder) and could see the phone was running away. It was going very fast and far away from our restaurant. When we called it, no one would pick up. What could we do? We prayed and commanded the angels to go find it!

We called the police, but they couldn't do anything for us. A little later, someone found our phone at a bus stop. What happened to the thief? I think an angel made the thief drop the iPhone at the bus stop, and they must have been scared and ran away. Then a "Good Samaritan" picked it up, called us, and gave the iPhone back. It was a miracle!

One way to activate our angels is to speak God's Word, because the angels go forth to do His Word.

——— Angels of God ———

Psalm 103:20

Bless the Lord, O you his angels, you mighty ones who DO HIS WORD, obeying the voice of his word!

Angels are God's servants, but they do not have to serve everybody. Angels minister to the "heirs of salvation".

Psalm 103:20

Bless the Lord, O you his angels,
you mighty ones who DO HIS WORD,
obeying the voice of his word!

Angels of God

Hebrews 1:13-14

13 And to which of the angels has he ever said, "Sit at my right hand until I make your enemies a footstool for your feet"? 14 Are they not all ministering spirits sent out to serve for the sake of those who are to inherit salvation?

Psalm 34:6

The angel of the Lord encamps around those who fear him, and delivers them.

One time my grandmother "Ya" and many of our friends were cleaning up her backyard garden. We filled up six big plastic bags full of leaves and twigs. The bags were so full no one could fit them in their car. She thought, "How will we get rid of them?" Then we went upstairs to eat and when we came down, all six plastic bags were gone! We looked and looked. Where could they have gone? No one would steal leaves and twigs! Even a truck could not take away so many. Angels came to clear her garden because my grandmother is always so busy serving Jesus, and angels are here to serve those who serve God.

🌺 7. Your Pastor 🌼

Jeremiah 3:15 (AKJV)

And I will give you pastors according to my heart, which shall feed you with knowledge and understanding.

My Papa is my pastor. People call him "Pastor Steve". Pastors say what God has spoken to them. It can be about water baptism, or about communion, or about end times. God speaks to them so you can know information from God, so you can know what God wants you to know!

If you want to have a good relationship with God, you should have a pastor. Without a pastor, people won't be able to do many things. And if you don't listen to the pastor, you will miss some information God wants to tell you, and you won't have a good life. Sometimes when I am not sure what to do, I know I can ask my pastor. When you feel sad or confused, you can talk to your pastor, and he can pray with you and tell you what God says.

Some kids I know moved out of church or out of Christian school because they don't like the pastor or principal. They say they just listen to God. God tells us to honor our father and mother, so we can't say we only listen to God. We also have to listen to our parents and we have to listen to other humans like our pastor. But some parents are not Christian, so they might tell you to do something God doesn't agree with, like worshipping idols or skipping church. How to know if your parents are Christian? They will read the Bible, pray to God, and not say bad things about pastors!

———— **Pastors** ————

1 Thessalonians 5:12-13

12 We ask you, brothers, to respect those who labor among you and are over you in the Lord and admonish you,
13 and to esteem them very highly in love because of their work. Be at peace among yourselves.

————————————

Pastors help us, but they also need our help. You can bless your pastor by praying for him or her, and taking them out for a nice meal or drinks!

8. Parents & Family

Parents will help you a lot. First of all, parents can read the Bible to you. If you want to learn the easy way, study the Bible, write memory verses, and listen to your parents. It says in the Bible, listen to your parents and honor them. Honor means to respect and do what the person says.

——— Parents ———

Ephesian 6:1-3

1 Children, obey your parents in the Lord, for this is right. 2 "Honor your father and mother" (this is the first commandment with a promise), 3 "that it may go well with you and that you may live long in the land."

Parents teach you to love your uncles, aunties, grandpa and grandma. They also help you to be polite, nice and kind to everyone. But you shouldn't follow everyone, especially if they are new people. Parents are wise because they've lived a long time, longer than children.

Proverbs 15:5 (GNT)

It is foolish to ignore what your parents taught you;
it is wise to accept their correction.

———————————

One day when you grow up, your parents may not be with you. You will still see them, but not all the time. So you have to listen to your heart and read the Bible every day. Then you will have a habit of it.

If you don't have any parent with you, but you're a Christian, God can still help you. God will be your Father and He will help you throughout your life just like a parent. When you go to church, God gives you a pastor to listen to. If you don't have your own church, you will meet a Christian who goes to church, then go to church and God will give you a pastor. But make sure it's a good church that doesn't allow anything bad that God does not like.

The most important thing about family is that your parents love you and you love your parents. I will tell you what love means soon (Chapter 12).

9. Animals

Animals are sent by God to help you or teach you something. They can be a pet or even toy animals. My toy bears help me face my fears and go to sleep in the dark. Penguins make me feel happy. Bunnies make me feel joyful.

My real dog is named "Reilly". He makes me happy. He helps me care for others because he is caring. I learn about obedience by watching him listen to commands we tell him.

I also learn about life because dogs do not live as long as humans. Reilly got old faster than us and when he was really old, he died. My Papa performed a funeral for him. We wrapped his body in a pretty towel and said "goodbye". Papa gave a Scripture, wept, and buried him in a special place.

——— Animals ———

Proverbs 12:10 (GNT)

Good people take care of their animals,
but wicked people are cruel to theirs.

Reilly gave me good times and showed me how to be good. I really miss him. When I play with him, he shows me examples of how to be nice. He is always joyful and cheerful. He is one of the best memories I've ever had. And he is a really good dog. He listens to what we say. He is very obedient. God has given us a very good dog.

You might like other animals. That's OK. When God spoke to Job, He spoke a lot about many kinds of animals, like oxen, ostriches, and eagles. Different animals remind us of different lessons from God.

—————— Animals ——————

Proverbs 6:6-9

6 Go to the ant, O sluggard; consider her ways, and be wise. 7 Without having any chief, officer, or ruler, 8 she prepares her bread in summer and gathers her food in harvest. 9 How long will you lie there, O sluggard? When will you arise from your sleep?

Ants don't wait to be told what they should do. They are hard-working. They go in groups to help each other. Ants teach us to work together and to never give up even if we're small. Elephants teach us to be obedient even if they're big. In India and Thailand, people say "come" and they come, "go" and they go, and humans can travel on their backs. Camels drink lots of water and can travel a long time without stopping. To be strong, you have to drink lots of water and never give up.

10. Evangelism

Another key that will help you have a good relationship with God is to evangelize. Evangelize just means telling other people about God. It gives you joy and it gives God joy. People in Heaven have a party when one new person comes to know God.

─────── **The Gospel** ───────

Luke 15:7

Just so, I tell you, there will be more JOY in HEAVEN over one sinner who repents than over ninety-nine righteous persons who need no repentance.

─────────────────────────

Our family loves to evangelize. Sometimes I walk or ride my bike and give out Christian flyers. We do this so more people can come to know God. We also do this so that when they learn about Jesus, they can tell their friends and family. We are very happy to do this. It's very special because of God and the flyers.

This is how my little brother gives out flyers. When we have a special event like a Christian movie night, he walks up to people near us and says, "Excuse me. Our church has a free movie night, would you like to come?" If they ask, "When is it?" or "Where is it?" he says, "It's on the flyer!" If they say, "OK, I'll come," then he smiles and says, "See you soon!" A Japanese and a Chinese person came to church because my brother gave them Christian flyers! It's so cool.

One time I invited a friend who doesn't know Jesus to church. I asked, "Would you like to come to church? To make new friends and know each other a little more?" And she said, "No, I have other important things." I was a little sad that she did not come to church, but next time, I will ask her, "What is more important than God?" I will just wait and see what she says. She might not have an answer because she doesn't know God yet. She might do whatever adults tell her and I am only a kid. But I pray that one day she will know God made her parents and her grandparents and everything. He is really the most important.

This is how you share the Gospel: "Have you ever done anything wrong, like lying or stealing or disobeying your parents?" Wait for your friend to answer, then explain: "When I do something wrong, I feel sad, because I hurt someone and I should be punished for doing wrong things. God sees we are in trouble. So God sent His Son Jesus to get us out of trouble. He was the only perfect Person. Jesus died for our sins, was buried, then rose again. If you believe what Jesus did for you and say with your own mouth that "He is Lord," you will be saved.

You can also share the Gospel in a really short way, like: "Did you know Jesus is the only One who can forgive your sins and take you to Heaven?" Or maybe you can ask them a question like, "Would you like to know God in your heart?" or "Would you like Jesus to help you get out of your trouble?"

FORGIVENESS PRAYER

When you need forgiveness, you can pray to God: "God, please forgive me for the bad things I have done. Thank You for sending Jesus to die for my sins and please write my name in the Your Book of Life, in Jesus' Name, Amen." Always pray "in Jesus' Name" because God listens to Jesus.

Let the little children come to me and do not hinder them, for to such belongs the kingdom of heaven.

Mark 7:27

Acts 2:21

…everyone who calls upon the name of the Lord
shall be saved.

————————————————————

Evangelism is one thing that is good to do
when you want to serve God. God is pleased with
evangelism.

11. Worship & Music

Worship

Daniel 6:10

...He got down on his knees three times a day
and prayed and gave thanks before his God,
as he had done previously.

Worship is the best thing you can do every morning. You can give praise to God or play music to Him. I like to do that. God is very pleased every time He hears us worshipping Him.

My favorite song is called "God Will Make a Way" by Don Moen. He also sings a nice song called "I Am the God that Healeth Thee." This song is good to listen to when you need healing. Christian music soothes your mind and helps you to think better. When you think better, it can help you listen to God and live a good life.

Worship

Psalm 100:1-4

1 Make a joyful noise to the Lord, all the earth!
2 Serve the Lord with gladness!
Come into his presence with singing!
3 Know that the Lord, he is God!
It is he who made us, and we are his;
we are his people, and the sheep of his pasture.
4 Enter his gates with thanksgiving, and his courts
with praise! Give thanks to him; bless his name!

I have a lot of music in my playlists. Most of my worship songs are really nice. I love to sing along with them or just listen to them. They help me think about God more. Instead of thinking of scary things or plots against people. It's nice to get calm with the music of the Lord. It is very joyful and helps you think straighter. You don't go crazy.

Some children listen a lot to music on YouTube and copy everything they do on the videos. They have fun for a short time but it doesn't help them. They act discombobulated. Parents and teachers even yell at them because they goof around too

much. Probably music changes their feelings. When I listen to my favorite Christian songs, I feel good and listen better.

─────── **Worship** ───────

Isaiah 38:20

The Lord will save me, and we will play my music on
stringed instruments all the days of our lives,
at the house of the Lord.

─────────────────────

I am starting to play to God on the piano. If kids learn an instrument, they can enjoy playing to God by themselves, then one day when they are bigger they might play on stage or at church. I know God enjoys it every time I play music to Him even though it might not sound very good yet.

12. The fruits of the Spirit

My favorite chapters in the Bible are Revelation 21, 1 Corinthians 13, and Galatians 5. I like Galatians chapter 5 because of the 9 fruits of the Spirit. Each fruit does something special which can help you. Each fruit can give you better relationships.

—————— Attitude ——————

Galatians 5:22-23 (NLT)

22 But the Holy Spirit produces this kind of fruit in our lives: love, joy, peace, patience, kindness, goodness, faithfulness, 23 gentleness, and self-control. There is no law against these things!

———————————————

God says nothing can be against these fruits (verse 23). That means even if people make fun of you or bully you, the fruits of the Spirit will help you. God is looking after you, so it doesn't matter about other people.

How do we get these fruits? First we must have the Holy Spirit inside us. Then like a plant, we have to grow till fruits come out. The more we grow close to God, the more fruits we have.

The Fruits of the Spirit

self control

gentleness

love

faithfulness

joy

peace

goodness

kindness

patience

When I know God loves me, it's easier to be loving to others. When I feel God's joy, I can be full of joy. God is peaceful, so when I'm with Him I feel peace. God is patient with us, so I can be patient with others. God is kind to me, so I want to be kind like Him. Every child should know God loves you very, very much. That's how you start growing in the fruits of the Spirit. These are all His fruits. He gives them to us when we spend time with Him.

I would like to tell you about the first and the last fruits: love and self-control. You can learn about the others at church or school. At the end of Year 2, all the students in my class had to memorize 1 Corinthians 13. It's the best chapter about love.

—————— **Love** ——————

1 Corinthians 13:2, 4-8 (Berean)

2 And if I have prophetic powers, and
understand all mysteries and all knowledge, and
if I have all faith, so as to remove mountains,
but have not love, I am nothing.
4 Love is patient, love is kind. It does not envy,
it does not boast, it is not proud.
5 It is not rude, it is not self-seeking, is not
easily angered, it keeps no account of wrongs.
6 Love takes no pleasure in evil,
but rejoices in the truth.
7 It bears all things, believes all things,
hopes all things, endures all things.
8 Love never fails…

————————————————

You can do great things but you must have love, otherwise all you did means nothing to God at all, because you did it so you could look good, get money or be famous. If you love someone you should help them, share with them, and also not be angry with them. You should not be rude to them. You should ask permission before you take, and if people ask you, you should share. You should not boast about yourself to someone else and say that you are better than them. If you boast, plot revenge or act rude to your friend, that is not having the fruit of love.

I can tell if someone really loves me by what they do even when they feel tired. They are still patient and they do not get rude even when they feel tired.

My Papa's Mama, I call her "Ya", is a very loving person. She always cooks nice food and is never rude. When my brother Austin and I visit her house, we often make a mess, but she is very patient. She doesn't yell and has a lot of self-control.

The ninth fruit of the spirit is self-control. I used to tell my little brother, "You have to self-control yourself!" Self-control means you feel like you really want to do it, but you don't; or you don't want to save something for next time, but you do. When you have the fruit of self-control, you can wait. Such as if you want ice-cream so badly that you cannot wait for next time, that is not self-control. But if you want it and can wait for it till next time, it can be nicer. If you wait for it, God might give you something better, even better than ice-cream!

Conclusion

There are 8 people who can help us through any difficulty: God the Father, Jesus God's Son, the Holy Spirit, angels, your pastor, parents, animals, and you. In this book, I put God first and you last.

Jesus gave us His Word, His Name, His Blood and His Body.

The Holy Spirit gave us His Power to pray, wisdom to evangelize and the nine fruits of the Spirit.

God the Father gave us fathers and mothers, pastors and teachers, animals and even angels.

God gave so many ways to defeat the devil and has so many people to help us, but we have to decide to worship God, evangelize and grow in the fruits of the Spirit, such as walking in love and practicing self-control. Sometime in your life, you may feel disappointed or "forget" to use some of these keys, but remember in life, it's not about how you start, but how you finish.

Never give up!

About the Author

My name is Steve Cioccolanti. I was born in Thailand to an Australian father and Thai mother. My last name means "chocolate maker" in Italian. My mother taught me to love books by taking me to bookstores. She sacrificed to buy me an Encyclopedia, before people had computers and could search for information on the Internet.

When I was 10 years old, our family moved to America. I was a shy kid and could not speak English well. With the help of my father and caring teachers, I not only became top of the class, but English became my favorite subject. I also enjoyed learning science, American history and European history. I went on to earn Bachelor and Masters degrees in universities.

After my education, I did not know what to do. I never dreamt I would write books others would read. My life changed when, back in Thailand, some people introduced me to Jesus Christ and prayed for me to be born again. I opened up my Bible for the first time and started reading Christian books. They were not like other books I had studied before. They were clear and could solve problems in my life.

I decided to study the Bible for real and graduated from a Bible school in America. From then on, the Lord sent me to 40 countries to preach the Gospel, teach the Bible and pray for the hurting. Over time, I gained experience and stories in helping people. Some of them were put into books. My other books include:

From Buddha to Jesus: An Insider's Perspective of Buddhism & Christianity.

The Divine Code from 1 to 2020: Numbers, Their Meanings & Patterns.

30 Days to a New You: Steps to Unshakable Faith & Freedom. (Great for teenagers!)

Having children also changed my life. Proverbs 22:6 says: "Train up a child in the way he should go…" Teaching them to grow up and be good people inspired me to be a better person. I like to spend my time reading to Alexis and Austin, taking our family on picnics, ski trips, and swimming. I also enjoy photography. If you're ever in Melbourne, Australia, I hope you will come visit my church.

To contact me, go to: **www.discover.org.au**

or watch me on

Youtube.com/DiscoverMinistries.

www.ingramcontent.com/pod-product-compliance
Lightning Source LLC
LaVergne TN
LVHW010025070426
835509LV00001B/15